And now God bless you; and all good union-men.

Yours as ever

A. Lincoln

From the photograph by Hesler, Chicago, 1860.

HERNDON'S LINCOLN

THE TRUE STORY OF A GREAT LIFE

Etiam in minimis major.

THE HISTORY AND PERSONAL RECOLLECTIONS

OF

ABRAHAM LINCOLN

BY

WILLIAM H. HERNDON

For Twenty Years His Friend and Law
Partner

AND

JESSE WILLIAM WEIK, A. M.

VOL. I.

CHICAGO, NEW YORK, AND SAN FRANCISCO
BELFORD, CLARKE & COMPANY
Publishers

London, HENRY J. DRANE, Lovell's Court, Paternoster Row

✦PREFACE✦

A QUARTER of a century has well-nigh rolled by since the tragic death of Abraham Lincoln. The prejudice and bitterness with which he was assailed have disappeared from the minds of men, and the world is now beginning to view him as a great historical character. Those who knew and walked with him are gradually passing away, and ere long the last man who ever heard his voice or grasped his hand will have gone from earth. With a view to throwing a light on some attributes of Lincoln's character heretofore obscure, and thus contributing to the great fund of history which goes down to posterity, these volumes are given to the world.

If Mr. Lincoln is destined to fill that exalted station in history or attain that high rank in the estimation of the coming generations which has been predicted of him, it is alike just to his memory and the proper legacy of mankind that the whole truth concerning him should be known. If the story of his life is truthfully and courageously told—nothing colored or suppressed; nothing false either written or suggested—the reader will see and feel the presence of the living man. He will, in fact, live with him and be moved to think and act

with him. If, on the other hand, the story is colored or the facts in any degree suppressed, the
reader will be not only misled, but imposed upon as
well. At last the truth will come, and no man need
hope to evade it.

"There is but one true history in the world,"
said one of Lincoln's closest friends to whom I con-
fided the project of writing a history of his life
several years ago, "and that is the Bible. It is
often said of the old characters portrayed there
that they were bad men. They are contrasted
with other characters in history, and much to the
detriment of the old worthies. The reason is, that
the Biblical historian told the whole truth—the
inner life. The heart and secret acts are brought
to light and faithfully photographed. In other his-
tories virtues are perpetuated and vices concealed.
If the life of King David had been written by an
ordinary historian the affair of Uriah would at most
have been a quashed indictment with a denial of
all the substantial facts. You should not forget
there is a skeleton in every house. The finest
character dug out thoroughly, photographed hon-
estly, and judged by that standard of morality or
excellence which we exact for other men is never
perfect. Some men are cold, some lewd, some dis-
honest, some cruel, and many a combination of all.
The trail of the serpent is over them all! Excellence consists, not in the absence of these attributes, but in the degree in which they are redeemed
by the virtues and graces of life. Lincoln's character will, I am certain, bear close scrutiny. I am

not afraid of you in this direction. Don't let anything deter you from digging to the bottom; yet
don't forget that if Lincoln had some faults, Washington had more—few men have less. In drawing
the portrait tell the world what the skeleton was
with Lincoln. What gave him that peculiar melancholy? What cancer had he inside?"

Some persons will doubtless object to the narra-
tion of certain facts which appear here for the first
time, and which they contend should have been
consigned to the tomb. Their pretense is that no
good can come from such ghastly exposures. To
such over-sensitive souls, if any such exist, my
answer is that these facts are indispensable to a full
knowledge of Mr. Lincoln in all the walks of life.
In order properly to comprehend him and the stir-
ring, bloody times in which he lived, and in which
he played such an important part, we must have all
the facts—we must be prepared to take him as he
was.

In determining Lincoln's title to greatness we
must not only keep in mind the times in which he
lived, but we must, to a certain extent, measure him
with other men. Many of our great men and our
statesmen, it is true, have been self-made, rising
gradually through struggles to the topmost round
of the ladder; but Lincoln rose from a lower depth
than any of them—from a stagnant, putrid pool, like
the gas which, set on fire by its own energy and
self-combustible nature, rises in jets, blazing, clear,
and bright. I should be remiss in my duty if I did
not throw the light on this part of the picture, so

that the world may realize what marvellous contrast one phase of his life presents to another.

The purpose of these volumes is to narrate facts, avoiding as much as possible any expression of opinion, and leaving the reader to form his own conclusions. Use has been made of the views and recollections of other persons, but only those known to be truthful and trustworthy. A thread of the narrative of Lincoln's life runs through the work, but an especial feature is an analysis of the man and a portrayal of his attributes and characteristics. The attempt to delineate his qualities, his nature and its manifestations, may occasion frequent repetitions of fact, but if truthfully done this can only augment the store of matter from which posterity is to learn what manner of man he was.

The object of this work is to deal with Mr. Lincoln individually and domestically; as lawyer, as citizen, as statesman. Especial attention is given to the history of his youth and early manhood; and while dwelling on this portion of his life the liberty is taken to insert many things that would be omitted or suppressed in other places, where the cast-iron rules that govern magazine writing are allowed to prevail. Thus much is stated in advance, so that no one need be disappointed in the scope and extent of the work. The endeavor is to keep Lincoln in sight all the time; to cling close to his side all the way through—leaving to others the more comprehensive task of writing a history of his times. I have no theory of his life to establish or destroy. Mr. Lincoln was my warm, devoted friend.

I always loved him, and I revere his name to this day. My purpose to tell the truth about him need occasion no apprehension ; for I know that "God's naked truth," as Carlyle puts it, can never injure the fame of Abraham Lincoln. It will stand that or any other test, and at last untainished will reach the loftiest niche in American history.

My long personal association with Mr. Lincoln gave me special facilities in the direction of obtaining materials for these volumes. Such were our relations during all that portion of his life when he was rising to distinction, that I had only to exercise a moderate vigilance in order to gather and preserve the real data of his personal career. Being strongly drawn to the man, and believing in his destiny, I was not unobservant or careless in this respect. It thus happened that I became the personal depositary of the larger part of the most valuable *Lincolniana* in existence. Out of this store the major portion of the materials of the following volumes has been drawn. I take this, my first general opportunity, to return thanks to the scores of friends in Kentucky, Indiana, Illinois, and elsewhere for the information they have so generously furnished and the favors they have so kindly extended me. Their names are too numerous for separate mention, but the recompense of each one will be the consciousness of having contributed a share towards a true history of the "first American."

Over twenty years ago I began this book; but an active life at the bar has caused me to postpone

the work of composition, until, now, being some-
what advanced in years, I find myself unable to
carry out the undertaking. Within the past three
years I have been assisted in the preparation of the
book by Mr. Jesse W. Weik, of Greencastle, Ind.,
whose industry, patience, and literary zeal have not
only lessened my labors, but have secured for him
the approbation of Lincoln's friends and admirers.
Mr. Weik has by his personal investigation greatly
enlarged our common treasure of facts and information. He has for several years been indefatigable
in exploring the course of Lincoln's life. In no
particular has he been satisfied with anything taken
at second hand. He has visited—as I also did in
1865—Lincoln's birthplace in Kentucky, his early
homes in Indiana and Illinois, and together, so to
speak, he and I have followed our hero continu-
ously and attentively till he left Springfield in 1861
to be inaugurated President. We have retained
the original MSS. in all cases, and they have never
been out of our hands. In relating facts therefore,
we refer to them in most cases, rather than to the
statements of other biographers.

This brief preliminary statement is made so that
posterity, in so far as posterity may be interested in
the subject, may know that the vital matter of this
narrative has been deduced directly from the consciousness, reminiscences, and collected data of

WILLIAM H. HERNDON.

SPRINGFIELD, ILL.,
    November 1, 1888.

CONTENTS.

CHAPTER I.

CHAPTER IV.

CHAPTER V.

CHAPTER VI.

CHAPTER VII.

CHAPTER VIII.

CHAPTER IX.

CHAPTER X.

CHAPTER XVII.

CHAPTER XVIII.

CHAPTER XIX.

CHAPTER XX.

APPENDIX.

THE LIFE OF LINCOLN.

CHAPTER I.

BEYOND the fact that he was born on the 12th day of February, 1809, in Hardin county, Kentucky, Mr. Lincoln usually had but little to say of himself, the lives of his parents, or the history of the family before their removal to Indiana. If he mentioned the subject at all, it was with great reluctance and significant reserve. There was something about his origin he never cared to dwell upon. His nomination for the Presidency in 1860, however, made the publication of his life a necessity, and attracted to Springfield an army of campaign biographers and newspaper men. They met him in his office, stopped him in his walks, and followed him to his house. Artists came to paint his picture, and sculptors to make his bust. His autographs were in demand, and people came long distances to shake him by the hand. This sudden elevation to national prominence found Mr. Lincoln unprepared in a great measure for the unaccustomed demonstrations that awaited him. While he was easy of approach and equally courteous to all,

yet, as he said to me one evening after a long day
of hand-shaking, he could not understand why
people should make so much over him.

Among the earliest newspaper men to arrive in
Springfield after the Chicago convention was the
late J. L. Scripps of the Chicago *Tribune*, who pro-
posed to prepare a history of his life. Mr. Lincoln
deprecated the idea of writing even a campaign
biography. "Why, Scripps," said he, "it is a great
piece of folly to attempt to make anything out of
me or my early life. It can all be condensed into a
single sentence, and that sentence you will find in
Gray's Elegy,

' The short and simple annals of the poor.'

That's my life, and that's all you or anyone else
can make out of it."

He did, however, communicate some facts and
meagre incidents of his early days, and, with the
matter thus obtained, Mr. Scripps prepared his
book. Soon after the death of Lincoln I received
a letter from Scripps, in which, among other things,
he recalled the meeting with Lincoln, and the view
he took of the biography matter.

"Lincoln seemed to be painfully impressed," he
wrote, "with the extreme poverty of his early surroundings, and the utter absence of all romantic
and heroic elements. He communicated some
facts to me concerning his ancestry, which he did
not wish to have published then, and which I have
never spoken of or alluded to before."

What the facts referred to by Mr. Scripps were

we do not know, for he died several years ago without, so far as is known, revealing them to anyone.

On the subject of his ancestry and origin I only remember one time when Mr. Lincoln ever referred to it. It was about 1850, when he and I were driving in his one-horse buggy to the court in Menard county, Illinois. The suit we were going to try was one in which we were likely, either directly or collaterally, to touch upon the subject of hereditary traits. During the ride he spoke, for the first time in my hearing, of his mother,* dwelling on her characteristics, and mentioning or enumerating what qualities he inherited from her. He said, among other things, that she was the illegitimate daughter of Lucy Hanks and a well-bred Virginia farmer or planter; and he argued that from this last source came his power of analysis, his logic, his mental activity, his ambition, and all the qualities that distinguished him from the other members and descendants of the Hanks family. His theory in discussing the matter of hereditary traits had been, that, for certain reasons, illegitimate children are oftentimes sturdier and brighter than those born in lawful wedlock; and in his case, he believed that his better nature and finer qualities came from this broad-minded, unknown Virginian. The revelation

---

*Dennis and John Hanks have always insisted that Lincoln's mother was not a Hanks, but a Sparrow. Both of them wrote to me that such was the fact. Their object in insisting on this is apparent when it is shown that Nancy Hanks was the daughter of Lucy Hanks, who *afterward* married Henry Sparrow. It will be observed that Mr. Lincoln claimed that his mother was a Hanks.

—painful as it was—called up the recollection of his mother, and, as the buggy jolted over the road, he added ruefully, "God bless my mother ; all that I am or ever hope to be I owe to her," * and immediately lapsed into silence. Our interchange of ideas ceased, and we rode on for some time without exchanging a word. He was sad and absorbed. Burying himself in thought, and musing no doubt over the disclosure he had just made, he drew round him a barrier which I feared to penetrate. His words and melancholy tone made a deep impression on me. It was an experience I can never forget. As we neared the town of Petersburg we were overtaken by an old man who rode beside us for awhile, and entertained us with reminiscences of days on the frontier. Lincoln was reminded of several Indiana stories, and by the time we had reached the unpretentious court-house at our destination, his sadness had passed away.

In only two instances did Mr. Lincoln over his own hand leave any record of his history or family descent. One of these was the modest bit of autobiography furnished to Jesse W. Fell, in 1859, in which, after stating that his parents were born in Virginia of "undistinguished or second families," he makes the brief mention of his mother, saying that she came " of a family of the name of Hanks." The

---

* If anyone will take the pains to read the Fell autobiography they will be struck with Lincoln's meagre reference to his mother. He even fails to give her maiden or Christian name, and devotes but three lines to her family. A history of the Lincolns occupies almost an entire page.

Thomas Lincoln, was born Jan 6th 1787 —
Abraham Lincoln, doct. &c. &c.
The [...] was born the Octo
13th 1809 —

Sarah Bush first married to
Daniel Johnston, was afterwards
married to Thomas Lincoln —
was born Feby 13th 1788 —
Daniel Johnston, doct. Mary &c.
Daniel Johnston, was born Mar
[...] to this [...]

Octobr 13th 1837 —
[...] Feby 2d 1816 —
Thomas D. Johnston, doct. [...]
Mary Johnston, was born [...]
[...] Johnston 10th 1837 —
Abraham D. W. Johnston [...]
doct. was born [...] 1838 —
[...] was born [...]
1840 —
Apriel 16 Johnston on [...]
[...] two December 15th 1841 —
[...] the [...]
[...] Octobr 31st 1843
[...] Johnston [...]
[...] Stevenson 18th 1845 —
[...] M. Johnston, born [...]
[...] born December 15th 1847 —
Nancy Jane Williard was born March
15 1856 —

Thomas Lincoln married to [...]
Johnston Nov 2d 1817 —
[...] died [...]
was married [...]
Aug [...] 1826 —

Abraham Lincoln, born [...] Mary
Lincoln was married to Mary
[...] Nov 4th 1842 —
John Johnston married to [...]
Sarah [...] Mary [...]
March 5 1781

John D. Johnston son
of John D. [...] and Mary
Jane Johnston [...] 1793
borne off April Nov 11 1834 —

1856
1810
46

1846
16
[...]

Nancy Lincoln, wife of [...] Lincoln
died Octobr 5th 1818
[...] Richard
[...] Cain by [...]
[...] Oct 12 1846 —

other record was the register of marriages, births,
and deaths which he made in his father's Bible.
The latter now lies before me. That portion of the
page which probably contained the record of the
marriage of his parents, Thomas Lincoln and Nancy
Hanks, has been lost; but fortunately the records
of Washington county, Kentucky, and the certifi-
cate of the minister who performed the marriage
ceremony—the Rev. Jesse Head—fix the fact and
date of the latter on the 12th day of June, 1806.

On the 10th day of February in the following year
a daughter Sarah * was born, and two years later,
on the 12th of February, the subject of these mem-
oirs came into the world. After him came the last
child, a boy—named Thomas after his father—who
lived but a few days. No mention of his existence
is found in the Bible record.

After Mr. Lincoln † had attained some prominence

---

* Most biographers of Lincoln, in speaking of Mr. Lincoln's sister,
call her Nancy, some—notably Nicolay and Hay—insisting that she
was known by that name among her family and friends. In this
they are in error. I have interviewed the different members of the
Hanks and Lincoln families who survived the President, and her
name was invariably given as Sarah   The mistake, I think, arises
from the fact that, in the Bible record referred to, all that portion relating to the birth of " Sarah, daughter of Thomas and Nancy Lincoln," down to the word Nancy has been torn away, and the latter
name has therefore been erroneously taken for that of the daughter.
Reading the entry of Abraham's birth below satisfies one that it
must refer to the mother.

† Regarding the paternity of Lincoln a great many surmises and
a still larger amount of unwritten or, at least, unpublished history
have drifted into the currents of western lore and journalism. A
number of such traditions are extant in Kentucky and other localities.
Mr. Weik has spent considerable time investigating the truth of a

in the world, persons who knew both himself and
his father were constantly pointing to the want of
resemblance between the two. The old gentleman
was not only devoid of energy, and shiftless, but
dull, and these persons were unable to account
for the source of his son's ambition and his intellectual superiority over other men. Hence the
charge so often made in Kentucky that Mr. Lincoln was in reality the offspring of a Hardin or a
Marshall, or that he had in his veins the blood of
some of the noted families who held social and
intellectual sway in the western part of the State.
These serious hints were the outgrowth of the
campaign of 1860, which was conducted with such
unrelenting prejudice in Kentucky that in the
county where Lincoln was born only six persons
could be found who had the courage to vote for
him.* I remember that after his nomination for

---

report current in Bourbon county, Kentucky, that Thomas Lincoln, for a consideration from one Abraham Inlow, a miller there,
assumed the paternity of the infant child of a poor girl named
Nancy Hanks; and, after marriage, removed with her to Washington
or Hardin county, where the son, who was named " Abraham, after
his real, and Lincoln after his putative, father," was born. A prominent citizen of the town of Mount Sterling in that state, who was at
one time judge of the court and subsequently editor of a newspaper,
and who was descended from the Abraham Inlow mentioned, has
written a long argument in support of his alleged kinship through
this source to Mr. Lincoln He emphasizes the striking similarity
in stature, facial features, and length of arms, notwithstanding the
well established fact that the first-born child of the real Nancy
Hanks was not a boy but a girl ; and that the marriage did not take
place in I ombon, but in Washington county.

* R. L. Wintersmith, of Elizabethtown, Kentucky.

the Presidency Mr. Lincoln received from Kentucky many inquiries about his family and origin. This curiosity on the part of the people in one who had attained such prominence was perfectly natural, but it never pleased him in the least ; in fact, to one man who was endeavoring to establish a relationship through the Hanks family he simply answered, "You are mistaken about my mother," without explaining the mistake or making further mention of the matter. Samuel Haycraft, the clerk of the court in Hardin county, invited him to visit the scenes of his birth and boyhood, which led him to say this in a letter, June 4, 1860 : * "You suggest that a visit to the place of my nativity might be pleasant to me. Indeed it would, but would it be safe? Would not the people lynch me?" That reports reflecting on his origin and descent should arise in a community in which he felt that his life was unsafe is by no means surprising. Abraham Lincoln,† the grandfather of the President, emigrated to Jefferson county, Kentucky, from Virginia about 1780, and from that time forward the former State became an important one in the history of the family, for in it was destined to be born its most illustrious member. About five years before this, a handful of Virginians had started across the

---

* Unpublished MS.

† Regarding the definition of the names " Lincoln " and " Hanks " it is said, the first is merely a local name without any special meaning, and the second is the old English diminutive of " Hal " or " Harry."

mountains for Kentucky, and in the company,
besides their historian, William Calk,—whose diary
recently came to light,—was one Abraham Hanks.
They were evidently a crowd of jolly young men
bent on adventure and fun, but their sport was
attended with frequent disasters.   Their journey
began at " Mr. Priges' tavern on the Rapidan."
When only a few days out " Hanks' Dog's leg got
broke."   Later in the course of the journey, Hanks
and another companion became separated from the
rest of the party and were lost in the mountains for
two days ; in crossing a stream "Abraham's saddle
turned over and his load all fell in Indian creek";
finally they meet their brethren from whom they
have been separated and then pursue their way
without further interruption.   Returning emigrants
whom they meet, according to the journal of Calk,
" tell such News of the indians " that certain members of the company are " afrade to go aney further."
The following day more or less demoralization
takes place among the members of this pioneer
party when the announcement is made, as their
chronicler so faithfully records it, that " Philip
Drake Bakes bread without washing his hands."
This was an unpardonable sin, and at it they
revolted.   A day later the record shows that
" Abram turns Back."   Beyond this we shall never
know what became of Abraham Hanks, for no further mention of him is made in this or any other
history.   He may have returned to Virginia and
become, for aught we know, one of the President's
ancestors on the maternal side of the house ; but if

so his illustrious descendant was never able to establish the fact or trace his lineage satisfactorily beyond the first generation which preceded him. He never mentioned who his maternal grandfather was, if indeed he knew.

His paternal grandfather, Abraham Lincoln,* the pioneer from Virginia, met his death within two years after his settlement in Kentucky at the hands of the Indians; " not in battle," as his distinguished grandson tells us, "but by stealth, when he was laboring to open a farm in the forest." The story of his death in sight of his youngest son Thomas, then only six years old, is by no means a new one to the world. In fact I have often heard the President describe the tragedy as he had inherited the story from his father. The dead pioneer had three sons, Mordecai, Josiah, and Thomas, in the order named. When the father fell, Mordecai, having hastily sent Josiah to the neighboring fort after assistance, ran into the cabin, and pointing his rifle through a crack between the logs, prepared for defense. Presently an Indian came stealing up to the dead father's body. Beside the latter sat the little boy Thomas. Mordecai took deliberate aim at a silver crescent which hung suspended from the Indian's breast, and brought him to the ground. Josiah returned from the fort with the desired relief, and

---

*"They [the Lincolns] were also called Linkhorns. The old settlers had a way of pronouncing names not as they were spelled, but rather, it seemed, as they pleased Thus they called Medcalf 'Medcap,' and Kaster they pronounced 'Custard.' "—MS. letter, Charles Friend, March 19, 1866.

the savages were easily dispersed, leaving behind one dead and one wounded.

The tragic death of his father filled Mordecai with an intense hatred of the Indians—a feeling from which he never recovered. It was ever with him like an avenging spirit. From Jefferson county he removed to Grayson, where he spent the remainder of his days. A correspondent * from there wrote me in 1865 : " Old Mordecai was easily stirred up by the sight of an Indian. One time, hearing of a few Indians passing through the county, he mounted his horse, and taking his rifle on his shoulder, followed on after them and was gone two days. When he returned he said he left one lying in a sink hole. The Indians, he said, had killed his father, and he was determined before he died to have satisfaction." The youngest boy, Thomas, retained a vivid recollection of his father's death, which, together with other reminiscences of his boyhood, he was fond of relating later in life to his children to relieve the tedium of long winter evenings. Mordecai and Josiah,† both remaining in Kentucky, became the heads of good-sized families, and although never known or

---

* W. T. Claggett, unpublished MS.

† " I knew Mordecai and Josiah Lincoln intimately. They were excellent men, plain, moderately educated, candid in their manners and intercourse, and looked upon as honorable as any men I have ever heard of Mordecai was the oldest son, and his father having been killed by the Indians before the law of primogeniture was repealed, he inherited a very competent estate. The others were poor. Mordecai was celebrated for his bravery, and had been in the early campaigns of the West."–Henry Pirtle, letter, June 17, 1865, MS.

heard of outside the limits of the neighborhoods in which they lived, were intelligent, well-to-do men. In Thomas, roving and shiftless, to whom was " reserved the honor of an illustrious paternity," are we alone interested. He was, we are told, five feet ten inches high, weighed one hundred and ninety-five pounds, had a well-rounded face, dark hazel eyes, coarse black hair, and was slightly stoop-shouldered. His build was so compact that Dennis Hanks used to say he could not find the point of separation between his ribs. He was proverbially slow of movement, mentally and physically ; was careless, inert, and dull ; was sinewy, and gifted with great strength ; was inoffensively quiet and peaceable, but when roused to resistance a danger-ous antagonist. He had a liking for jokes and stories, which was one of the few traits he trans-mitted to his illustrious son ; was fond of the chase, and had no marked aversion for the bottle, though in the latter case he indulged no more freely than the average Kentuckian of his day. At the time of his marriage to Nancy Hanks he could neither read nor write ; but his wife, who was gifted with more education, and was otherwise his mental supe-rior, taught him, it is said, to write his name and to read—at least, he was able in later years to spell his way slowly through the Bible. In his relig-ious belief he first affiliated with the Free-Will Baptists. After his removal to Indiana he changed his adherence to the Presbyterians—or Predestina-rians, as they were then called—and later united with the Christian—vulgar'y called Campbellite—

Church, in which latter faith he is supposed to have died. He was a carpenter by trade, and essayed farming too ; but in this, as in almost every other undertaking, he was singularly unsuccessful. He was placed in possession of several tracts of land at different times in his life, but was never able to pay for a single one of them. The farm on which he died was one his son purchased, providing a life estate therein for him and his wife. He never fell in with the routine of labor ; was what some people would call unfortunate or unlucky in all his business ventures—if in reality he ever made one—and died near the village of Farmington in Coles county, Illinois, on the 17th day of January, 1851. His son, on account of sickness in his own family, was unable to be present at his father's bedside, or witness his death. To those who notified him of his probable demise he wrote : " I sincerely hope that father may yet recover his health ; but at all events tell him to remember to call upon and confide in our great and good and merciful Maker, who will not turn away from him in any extremity. He notes the fall of a sparrow, and numbers the hairs of our heads ; and He will not forget the dying man who puts his trust in him. Say to him that if we could meet now it is doubtful whether it would not be more painful than pleasant ; but that if it be his lot to go now he will soon have a joyous meeting with the many loved ones gone before, and where the rest of us, through the help of God, hope ere long to join them." *

* MS. letter to John Johnston. Jan. 12, 1851.

Nancy Hanks, the mother of the President, at a very early age was taken from her mother Lucy— afterwards married to Henry Sparrow—and sent to live with her aunt and uncle, Thomas and Betsy Sparrow. Under this same roof the irrepressible and cheerful waif, Dennis Hanks *—whose name will be frequently seen in these pages—also found a shelter. At the time of her marriage to Thomas Lincoln, Nancy was in her twenty-third year. She was above the ordinary height in stature, weighed about 130 pounds, was slenderly built, and had much the appearance of one inclined to consumption. Her skin was dark; hair dark brown; eyes gray and small; forehead prominent; face sharp and angular, with a marked expression of melancholy which fixed itself in the memory of everyone who ever saw or knew her. Though her life was seemingly beclouded by a spirit of sadness, she was in disposition amiable and generally cheerful. Mr. Lincoln himself said to me in 1851, on receiving the news of his father's death, that whatever might be said of his parents, and however unpromising the early surroundings of his mother may have been, she was highly intellectual by nature, had a strong memory, acute judgment, and was cool and heroic. From a mental standpoint she no doubt rose above her surroundings, and had she lived, the stimulus of

---

* Dennis Hanks, still living at the age of ninety years in Illinois, was the son of another Nancy Hanks—the aunt of the President's mother. I have his written statement that he came into the world through nature's back-door. He never stated, if he knew it, who his father was.

her nature would have accelerated her son's success, and she would have been a much more ambitious prompter than his father ever was.

As a family the Hankses were peculiar to the civilization of early Kentucky. Illiterate and superstitious, they corresponded to that nomadic class still to be met with throughout the South, and known as " poor whites." They are happily and vividly depicted in the description of a camp-meeting held at Elizabethtown, Kentucky, in 1806, which was furnished me in August, 1865, by an eye-witness.* "The Hanks girls," narrates the latter, "were great at camp-meetings. I remember one in 1806. I will give you a scene, and if you will then read the books written on the subject you may find some apology for the superstition that was said to be in Abe Lincoln's character. It was at a camp-meeting, as before said, when a general shout was about to commence. Preparations were being made ; a young lady invited me to stand on a bench by her side where we could see all over the altar. To the right a strong, athletic young man, about twenty-five years old, was being put in trim for the occasion, which was done by divesting him of all apparel except shirt and pants. On the left a young lady was being put in trim in much the same manner, so that her clothes would not be in the way, and so that, when her combs flew out, her hair would go into graceful braids. She, too, was young—not more than twenty perhaps. The per-

---

* J. B. Helm, MS.

SARAH BUSH LINCOLN

After photograph in author's possession

DENNIS HANKS

DR. E. H. MERRYMAN.

GEORGE W. SHUTT.

RICHARD YATES.

EDW" W. McGAUGHEY.

WILLIAM BUTLER

Wᴹ J. FERGUSON. STEPHEN T. LOGAN.

EDWARD BAKER.

N.M.BROADWELL J.C.CONKLING.

SPRINGFIELD—U. S. COURT BUILDING, 1850-1860. LOGAN & LINCOLN'S LAW OFFICE, THIRD STORY

After recent photograph

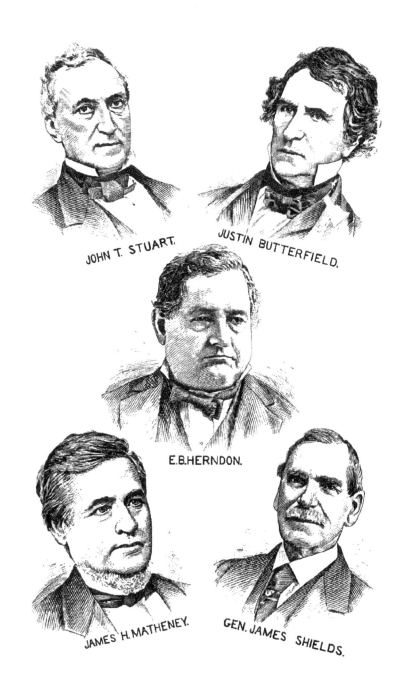

JOHN T. STUART.   JUSTIN BUTTERFIELD.

E.B.HERNDON.

JAMES H.MATHENEY.   GEN. JAMES SHIELDS.

HOUSE IN WHICH THOMAS LINCOLN DIED, NEAR FARMINGTON, COLES COUNTY, ILL.

After recent photograph

E. C. Ross

To Stuart & Lincoln   Dr

1837 — April — To attendance at trial of right of
J. F. Davis's property before Moffett $ 5.00

Matter, Lamb & Co

To Stuart & Lincoln   Dr

1837 — April. To attendance at trial of right of
J. F. Davis' property before Moffett $ 5.00

Lucinda Mason

To Stuart & Lincoln   Dr

1837 Oct To obtaining assignment of Dower. $5.00,

Wiley & Wood

To Stuart & Lincoln   Dr

1837-8   To defence of Chancery case of Ely $ 50-00
Credit by Cost to Stuart —   15-00
                                             $ 35-00

Peyton L. Harrison

To Stuart & Lincoln   Dr.

1838 — March — To case with Dickinson — $ 10-00.

Allen & Stone

To. Stuart & Lincoln   Dr

1838 Oct   To case with Cantor, $2.50

A PAGE FROM STUART & LINCOLN'S FEE BOOK
Entries written by Abraham Lincoln

(Slightly reduced)

SPRINGFIELD—RESIDENCE OF NINIAN W. EDWARDS

House in which Lincoln and Mary Todd were married, and in which the latter died

After photograph taken in November, 1886

THIS CABINET
WAS MADE BY
ABRAHAM LINCOLN
WHILE A RESIDENT OF
SPENCER COUNTY IND

WALNUT CABINET MADE BY THOMAS AND ABRAHAM LINCOLN
After photograph in possession of owner, J. W. Wartmann, Esq.

THE CRAWFORD HOME, SPENCER COUNTY, IND.

Photographed in 1865

Subtraction of Long Mea[sure]

L	M	f	P
7	1	3	10
44	2	5	16
21	1	5	34
11	1	3	10

Subr

Y	f	F	B
48	0	4	2
12	0	3	1
36	0	10	1
48	0	1	2

# of Land Measure

A	R	P	
			40
12	1	10	
5	3	17	
6	1	33	
12	1	10	

A	R	P	
		4	40
17	3	14	
12	3	23	
4	3	34	
17	3	14	

a	r	h	
		4	40
28	1	4	
19	1	28	
8	3	19	
28	1	7	

# of Dry Measure

Ch	B	P	
		36	4
17	2	1	
10	1	3	
7	0	2	
17	2	1	

C	Ch		
		36	4
40	1	2	
16	5	1	
23	32	1	
40	1	2	

9	B	P	
		8	2
19	1	1	
12	4	2	
6	1	3	
19	1	1	

Abraham Lincoln
his hand and pen
he will be good but
god knows When

SPRINGFIELD, 1839—FIRST COURT-HOUSE. STUART & LINCOLN'S OFFICE, UPPER STORY, OVER FURNITURE STORE

After photograph by D. J. Ryan, 1888

HON. MILTON. HAY.

JNO E. ROSETT.

DAVID. LOGAN.

JUDGE CHAS S. ZANE.

S.M. CULLOM

JOSHUA F. SPEED AND WIFE

After oil-painting in possession of family

LINCOLN MONUMENT—SPRINGFIELD, ILL.
GROUPS OF STATUARY AND SARCOPHAGUS

WASHINGTON—FORD'S THEATRE

Photographed by J. F. Jarvis

LINCOLN'S TOMB, OAK RIDGE CEMETERY, SPRINGFIELD

After photograph, 1884

WASHINGTON—THE PETERSON HOUSE

GEN. JOHN M. PALMER

After photograph by Pittman, Springfield, Ill.

MRS. LINCOLN IN THE WHITE HOUSE

After a photograph by Brady, 1861

INTERIOR VIEW OF LINCOLN'S PARLOR, SPRINGFIELD RESIDENCE

After a recent photograph

MARY TODD LINCOLN

After a photograph from life

LINCOLN & HERNDON'S LAW OFFICE IN 1860

After a recent photograph

Springfield—Old State House, New Sangamon County Court-House

LINCOLN AS HE APPEARED DURING THE DEBATE WITH DOUGLAS

After an ambrotype taken by C. Jackson, at Pittsfield, Illinois, Oct. 1, 1858

FIRST PRESBYTERIAN CHURCH, SPRINGFIELD

After photograph taken in September, 1888

STEPHEN A. DOUGLAS

Your Friend
W. H. Herndon

DAVID DAVIS

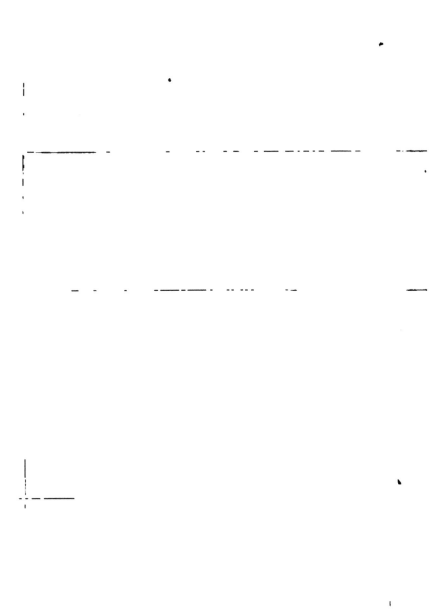

Prospectus

Printed in the USA
CPSIA information can be obtained
at www.ICGtesting.com
LVHW020858170124
769040LV00006B/276